SOUL JOURNEY
THROUGH
RAHU & KETU

VIMLESHWARI SINGH

BLUEROSE PUBLISHERS
India | U.K.

Copyright © Vimleshwari Singh 2024

All rights reserved by author. No part of this publication may be reproduced, stored in a retrieval system or transmitted in any form or by any means, electronic, mechanical, photocopying, recording or otherwise, without the prior permission of the author. Although every precaution has been taken to verify the accuracy of the information contained herein, the publisher assumes no responsibility for any errors or omissions. No liability is assumed for damages that may result from the use of information contained within.

BlueRose Publishers takes no responsibility for any damages, losses, or liabilities that may arise from the use or misuse of the information, products, or services provided in this publication.

For permissions requests or inquiries regarding this publication, please contact:

BLUEROSE PUBLISHERS
www.BlueRoseONE.com
info@bluerosepublishers.com
+91 8882 898 898
+44 07342 408967

ISBN: 978-93-6261-294-6

Cover design: Rishav Rai
Typesetting: Rohit

First Edition: May 2024

About the Author

...

Vimleshwari, the insightful author of this book, delves deep into ancient sciences to explore the intricate relationship between cosmic energies and human life. Her journey from being a postgraduate in Chemistry to a seasoned teacher reflects her thirst for knowledge beyond the mundane.

Fascinated by how the universe interplays with our existence, Vimleshwari's exploration led her to unravel the mysteries of soul growth and reincarnation. Through her expertise as an astrovastu expert and astrologer, she bridges the gap between celestial forces and earthly experiences, shedding light on the profound concept of soul evolution.

Her profound understanding of higher realms, akashic records, and angel therapies showcases her dedication to unlocking spiritual insights for personal transformation. Vimleshwari's work serves as a guiding beacon for those seeking enlightenment amidst life's cosmic dance.

Vimleshwari brings a unique perspective on aligning life for the growth of the soul. By spreading awareness about utilising astrology as a tool for understanding and enhancing life's journey, she empowers individuals to tap into their cosmic energies for personal development and spiritual growth.

Astrology serves as a powerful guide in Vimleshwari's teachings, shedding light on how planetary influences can shape our paths and illuminate opportunities for soulful evolution. Through her insights and wisdom, readers are inspired to explore the depths of their being, align with their true purpose, and navigate life with clarity and intention toward greater fulfilment.

Introduction

...

This book is all about life, your life, my life, and everyone's life whosoever has chosen earth for life. Have you ever wondered why are you born into a particular family? Why not some other family? Why do you have a gender of a female, not a male, or vice versa? Why someone is a born genius while someone is born insane? Why do you have a healthy body while some are born with genetic defects?

There are so many questions that might be arising in your mind often and on but where is the answer? Can someone answer many unresolved queries or does science also has its limits?

We are going to talk about many things that might relate to you or maybe to someone known to you.

In astrology (Jyotish), we can find answers to many unresolved questions. You have the full right to know about your life.

The body which is yours, was so small when you were born and then it grew up with time. You were in the womb of your mother but the question is why you were present in her womb and not in someone else's. This is a very mysterious question.

Vedic Jyotish(Astrology) can talk about your roots, your genes, your past life, your life purpose and much more.

Your body which is very active at this moment will be dead if the prana energy is gone. Your soul is the real you and is the main energy source of life.

Body + Soul = Active body

A soul without a body and a body without a soul is of no use on this planet Earth but the major difference is that the soul has an identity in a separate world i.e. the soul world while the body is of no use without the soul.

The day a soul decides to grow It decides to come on earth and incarnate as a human body. But why does it take such a decision? Because it wants to grow and the fast growth is only possible on Earth. The ultimate goal of the soul is to become one with the Supreme Soul or God. And that is only possible once it has has learned all the lessons.

Each time the soul takes birth It creates many karmas. The soul chooses its family on earth, especially the mother. The family you are born in, is your choice because your soul knows that whatever conditions are required for you to grow can only be provided initially via the family you are going to be part of. And sometimes it has pending karmas of that family tree.

The soul itself chooses the hardships of life as a means to grow. However, once it takes birth and incarnates as a human, its conscious brain takes over subconscious mind and we forget what our soul's purpose is and why it chose such conditions. Our subconscious mind becomes dormant and we start blaming God and others for our hardships because we completely forget our life and our soul's purpose.

Now the question arises how can we understand our life purpose and our roots? Astrology can help you with this. You must be aware that astrology talks about nine planets namely the Sun, Moon, Mercury, Mars, Jupiter, Venus, Saturn, Rahu, and Ketu. Out of these nine planets, Rahu (North Node of the Moon) and Ketu (South Node of the Moon) can help you reveal many mysteries of your present life and past life connection to this life. Let us try to unveil your life through these two planets.

Contents

...

KETU and your Past Life..1
Ketu in the first house..4
Ketu in the second house..6
Ketu in the Third House...8
Ketu in the Fourth House 10
Ketu in the Fifth House...13
Ketu in the Sixth House..15
Ketu in Seventh House 17
Ketu in the Eighth House..19
Ketu in the Ninth House 21
Ketu in the Tenth House 23
Ketu in the Eleventh House...25
Ketu in the Twelfth House..27
Rahu and Your Present Life...29
Rahu in the First House 32
Rahu in the Second House 34
Rahu in the Third House 36
Rahu in the Fourth House...38
Rahu in Fifth House..40

Rahu in the Sixth House 42
Rahu in the Seventh House 44
Rahu in the Eighth House 46
Rahu in Ninth House 48
Rahu in the Tenth House 50
Rahu in the Eleventh House 52
Rahu in the Twelfth House 54
Conclusion 56

KETU and your Past Life

...

Ketu, the South node of the Moon is all about your roots lying in the past. Past of this life as well as your previous life. Ketu is past. Ketu is roots. Ketu is the foundation. Ketu is your past life karma. You cannot get rid of your past, because the past has led to the foundation of your present. Unless you understand your past, release the pain of the past, and get rid of the baggage of deeds that you are carrying from the past, you can't grow as a soul no matter what you do.

This life is 40% past and 60% present. The universe has given you a 60% chance to write your new journey, but 40% of your life is based on your past life karma, and you can't get away from it. Imagine how rapidly you can grow if you choose to rectify and clean the past baggage. It's just like unloading a heavy bag at your back and walking freely.

Ketu can help you in this process. Let us understand what is Ketu.

Ketu signifies the following:-

- Contraction
- Detachment
- Roots
- Foundation
- Grounded
- Fear
- Pain
- Subconscious mind
- Inward journey
- Straight
- Spirituality

Wherever Ketu is placed in your birth chart or ascendant chart, that is the place that contains your past life karma that need to be resolved. You have already utilised the attributes of that place in your past life and all the karma you developed in the past life were through these attributes only. Unless you resolve them, you can't grow. Further in this book, we will talk about your life journey in previous birth and what karma you have to resolve in this life. Understand Ketu in different houses of birth chart and find out by yourself, what is your karmic knot that needs to be opened.

Before we start our journey to understand the planet in different houses of birth chart let us understand what do we mean by houses in birth chart. Look at given figure . It has 12 partition ,each segment is known as a HOUSE. House is fixed but the number in the house can change because number denotes zodiac in that house.eg.1st house can have number 5 written in it but it will still be the 1st house.Number 5 will denote that 1st house has 5th zodiac (Leo) residing there.

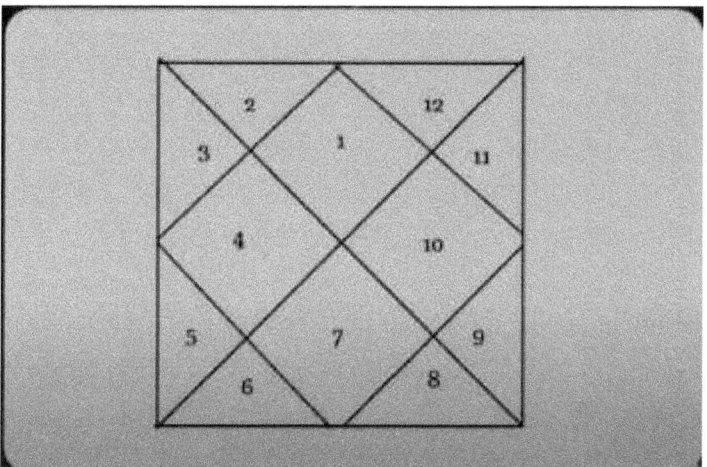

Ketu in the first house

...

The first house of the horoscope is 'You' ie SELF. It depicts your personality as well as your outer appearance.

When Ketu is placed in the first house of Lagan Kundli or the ascendant birth chart, it indicates that in the previous birth, you have led a life fully focused on yourself. You might have been a very self-centred person, a person who was too much involved in the building of the self or personality. Ketu in the house of self indicates that your karmic knot is related to yourself. In this birth, you may have to deal with lots of personality issues. In the past, you might have ignored your partner as you were too much involved in yourself.

If this is your placement, you have to be aware, that the more you focus on yourself, the more you will have to face the consequences. You need to understand partnership and try to create harmony and balance with your partner. You should be aware that the personality issues you are facing in this life are your life lessons due to your karmic deeds of the past.

As Ketu is a contraction, it will not let you pay attention to the flaws in your personality as you're completely detached from yourself. Ketu demands an inward journey, but this placement in the first house will not let you go inward, rather you will be looking outward only. Ketu can also make you careless towards yourself.

The more you focus on your behaviour, accept your flaws, and try to glorify yourself from within, the faster you will grow in this life.

Ketu in the second house

...

Let's first understand what is the second house in the birth chart and then only we can understand what is Ketu demanding from us in the second house.

The second house represents the following:-

1. Our immediate family.

2. Our family values.

3. Our savings as in a bank which is liquid cash or movable property.

4. Our speech(voice)

5. Our food taste, etc.

When Ketu resides in the second house, one must understand that your immediate family has something to do with your past life. Your karmic knot is about family values. You might have been involved in actions that your family didn't approve of or maybe you lived family life to the fullest and that's why there is a possibility of mistakes being made in that arena of life.

Ketu is contraction so in this life either you don't have an immediate family or you may have a family but at some point in life, you may have to face a situation where you will have to detach yourself from them. Your karmic knots lie in your family values. So you need to be conscious about how you are dealing with your immediate family members or family values.

As it is the house of food, you could have been a very foodie person in the past and never paid attention to the choice of food you are eating, your focus was eating, so this time you might be detached from food and might eat whatever you get. Pay attention to your eating habits as they may create health concerns for you.

Your savings can be problematic in this life. A time can come when you will be running short of money. Your bank balance may run out at some stage of life.

You have to understand that keeping money in the bank and not helping the needy is wrong. Understand the value of money. The day you understand the real meaning of money, the real meaning of food and overcome your karmic knot, real joy will come to you.

Ketu in the Third House

...

To understand Ketu in the third house of the birth chart, you will have to connect with the attributes of the third house with the qualities of Ketu.

The third house represents the following:-

1. Communication.

2. Social media.

3. Younger siblings.

4. Short travels.

5. Your efforts, valour, courage.

6. Relatives, Neighbours, office colleagues.

When the planet of detachment sits in the house of younger siblings it indicates that either you do not have younger siblings or if you have them then their presence in your life is negligible. Either they live very far away from you or a stage will come in life when you may become detached from your younger siblings.

This placement of Ketu indicates that in the previous life, you had shown a lot of effort for gains and as a result, you have created karmic debts related to it.

The third house is also the house of communication so watch out the way you communicate with others. Your harsh language might hurt people and will create more karmas. This placement of Ketu demands that you understand the value of communication. Your communication should not hurt other people. You need to forgive your younger siblings. Forgiveness doesn't mean you need to be attached too much, rather it means not to keep the feeling of hatred or harshness inside your heart. You just need to move on.

You need to create a balance and harmony as you are experienced in that quality. Utilise that experience instead of getting stuck with Ketu.

It is necessary to live with the quality of letting go and clear your karmas. Do not let the grief or resentment of any situation stay in your heart. Else those feelings will be carried forward by Ketu in your next birth.

Ketu in the Fourth House

...

When we talk about Ketu in the fourth house, remember it is one of the most difficult placements to deal with.

The fourth house of the birth chart is

1- Your mother.

2- Immovable property like home, vehicle, luxuries of life etc.

3- Happiness within your heart.

4- Your homely happiness.

5- Educational institute.

Remember, no matter how wealthy or successful and rich you are unless you have happiness within, all the things you acquire are useless because we humans want to achieve everything for happiness. Ketu sitting in the fourth house says that you has already experienced all luxuries and property in the previous birth. Ketu is asking you not to fall into the trap of that emotion of greed or hunger for these things else you will get stuck.

It is not asking you not to acquire all these things again rather it is asking you not to get too much attached to them.

Generally, it is seen that people with this placement of Ketu have all the luxurious items in their lives. However, they are not running after them. There is a feeling of detachment from all these items depending upon the past life. If your karma were too bad, then you could be completely devoid of these attributes of the fourth house. So if you do not have a home, luxuries, vehicles, etc in your life and Ketu is placed in the fourth house then it is a matter of deep concern. You must try to analyse yourself. Are you running too much after materialism? Are you trying to find happiness in materialism? Are you completely unaware of the spiritual journey of your own? If that's the case with you then you need to rethink about your life as you are completely on the wrong track. Ketu in the fourth house is trying to tell you that attain luxuries but do not get indulged too much in them. The day you will start your journey within and create the balance within yourself you will realise that whatever you are running after has finally started coming your way because now you have untied your karmic knot.

Another important lesson related to the fourth house is issues with your mother. Either mother is missing from your life or if she is there then her life conditions might be such that she may not be available to fulfil your demands or you may be devoid of her motherly affection. Her busy routine can keep you missing her presence in your life. In the fourth house, Ketu can create a situation in your life when you might feel detached from your mother because you are carrying karmic issues from the past related to your mother.

If you want to attain happiness and growth of your soul in this birth, then learn to let go of whatever is bothering you related to her. Fulfil your duties towards her and do not demand a payback for your acts. Once you start doing this, you will realise that your past life karmic knot is opening and your life will start to change magically. That missing happiness will start coming to you. And you will feel happy from within.

Ketu in the Fifth House

...

Understanding the fifth house can help you understand what is the role of Ketu in your life. The fifth house represents the following:-

1- House of Past life.

2- Children

3- Emotions.

4- Intellect.

5- Creativity.

6- Entertainment industry

7- House of a love affair(romantic life)

Ketu is a planet of detachment and contraction, sitting in the house of children. It can indicate that you have brought forward issues related to children in this birth. You had developed karmas in the past that are deeply connected to children. If your deeds were not good then there is a possibility that you will be devoid of kids in this birth. But even if you have kids then be sure you will have to deal with certain severe issues related with them as your issues with them are seated in past Life. A feeling of detachment will come up at some stage of life due to some unavoidable situation. But you need to understand that if you deal with kids, keeping a thought in your mind that all the problems that you are receiving through them are due to the past and try to resolve these issues with them by letting go of your ego, then situations related to your kids will change. Things will start to fall in the right place. You need to deal with your own emotions, rather than expecting others to fulfil your emotions. The sooner you understand the exact meaning of emotions , the faster you will align your life.

Another meaning of this placement is that past life issues are very prominent. When Ketu sits in the fifth house there is no shortcut or no running away. Learn to deal with your emotions. There is a great need for you to understand that one has to stop at some point else this will never let you have emotional stability. It wants to teach you to ground your emotions. There is no midway here.

Romance is missing in your life, understand love, the real love is not outer it is about taking care of the emotions of others as well.If you want love in your life then be ready to deal with emotions.Ketu has made you a person who is detached from emotions and you are running for fulfilment of your desire.Learn to create a balance between love and desires.

Ketu in the Sixth House

...

The sixth house represents

1- Daily life struggles.

2- It is the house of competitions.

3- Your competitive spirit and daily life.

4- Challenges in life.

5- Short term disease.

6- Litigation and court case.

7- Hidden enemies.

8- Loans, debts.

9- medication.

10- services.

Ketu's placement here can make you a person who does not want to deal with the situations provided by the sixth house.

You might not want to face competitions or might get nervous at the approach of any kind of challenge or competition. You rather want to stay away from litigations or it is really hard for you to digest those litigations, although you will not have to face too many enemies in life as this house has the energy of Ketu and Ketu is contraction.

At the time of real requirement, you might not be able to use your strength against your enemy

The sixth house is also the house of services you provide to the society. When Ketu is placed here, you might not be interested in providing any services to the society.

But Ketu has a karmic knot here. It wants you to deal with what you don't want to. It is recommended to do social service to clear your past life debt.

Learn not to run away from challenges , rather face them.

Ketu in Seventh House

...

Ketu's placement in the seventh house is very interesting.

The seventh house represents the following:-

1- Your life partner.

2- Your legal partner,.

3- Your business partner.

4- House of business.

When the energy of Ketu is in this house, your married life is really difficult as you have a karmic knot with your partner. You have pending karmas related to your partner which you will have to deal with. You may not get the right partner if the karmas were too bad and even if you have a partner then there is a sense of detachment. A point will come in your life when your partner will detach from you and will leave you. Your married life is at stake with Ketu in the seventh house.

It all depends on you whether you want to change the situations related to your married life or not.

You will have to put extra effort to create harmony in your relationship. You will have to let go of your ego related to partnerships and ground yourself. Release the issues and learn to forgive. You need to be compassionate towards your partner and try to understand his or her demands or requirements as well. The more you stay detached from your partner and become self-centred the more severe the consequences you will invite in your life.

But the day you start understanding that there is always two-way traffic in partnership, your life situation will change for good in your married life.

Be compassionate for your partner don't be over demanding.

No matter what energy one brings from the past their is always a possibility to change anything through sincere efforts. That is why we say "Man is the maker of it's own destiny"

Past life karma brings event and situations in our life But reaction is purely ours and through our reactions we can change the results.It is all about our awareness.And Astrology can help to create that awareness in you.

Ketu in the Eighth House

...

To understand what kind of energy Ketu is bringing into your life through the eighth house, you must first understand what exactly is the eighth house in the birth chart.

Eight houses represent the following:-

1-Sudden loss and sudden gains.

2- Unearned money.

3- Parental inheritance.

4- Long-term Chronic diseases.

5- Scandals.

6- Research.

7- Occult and astrology.

8- In-laws.

The eighth house is like a dark place where nothing is visible and anything can come up all of a sudden, as a surprise.

Ketu Believes in digging deep into the ground. So there is no doubt that from the research point of view, it is a very good placement as you are well versed in research from past life.

Study of the occult or astrology or any kind of scientific/occult research can be beneficial for people with Ketu in the eighth house.

But Ketu in the eighth house can also give you a feeling of fear of the unknown.

Meditation can help people with such placement as it can help you dive deep and then gain the power to research in your required field.

As this is the house of in-laws, so there is a possibility that you might get married to a person who is living far away from his parents and hence the involvement of in-laws in your life will be minimal or you might not have in-laws but if you have then at one stage of life, you will have to deal with a challenging situation created by them in your life. The more you understand the workings of Ketu shed off your ego let go of the issue that is involved concerning in-laws and become compassionate towards them and easier the situation will become as you will be able to free yourself from the karmic debt of the past life. Ketu contracts the energy of the house where it is placed. So it is good to have Ketu in a challenging house as it will minimise the negative effects of that house in your life, but only if you walk hand and hand with Ketu, fulfilling its demands when required as it has the keys to open the pathway for your soul growth.

Ketu in the Ninth House

...

Ketu is roots and the ninth house is the house of Dharma and religious beliefs. So Ketu will make such a person attached to one's religion and follow its religious beliefs faithfully.Or Possibility of complete detachment with Dharm.(Religion)

The ninth house is the house of teachers, gurus, and father. Hence, you can have your karmic knots related to your teachers, father, or religion.

The ninth house represents the following:-

1- Belief system.

2- Father.

3-Teachers.

4-Wisdom.

5-Higher studies.

6-Foreign travel.

7-Air travel, etc.

8- Religious Philosophy.

If Ketu is placed in the ninth house then it is possible that you acquired higher education in your past life and had attained wisdom, but despite that, you might have done some sins which were least expected from a highly learned person. There is a chance that you might have disrespected your teachers or father even after acquiring knowledge and wisdom or might have done things that were against the religious belief system. That is why your Ketu is placed in the ninth house.

What you have to understand is that ,in this life, you might encounter issues with your father or teachers. Support system from them might not be available to you and even if the support system is available, there will come at least one situation in your life where you will be facing challenges related with them. That will detach you from them.

You need to work following Ketu. Shedding off your ego and letting it go in severe situations. Ketu teaches us to shed off selfishness and to become selfless.

If you work in accordance with Ketu's learning, then your soul growth will become unstoppable. Because Ketu is detachment, you might not be too much involved in religious activities. It is always good for this placement of Ketu that one should stay rooted and connected with their culture no matter what they are doing.

Ketu in the Tenth House

...

When Ketu is placed in the tenth house of your horoscope, it is a very unique kind of placement because, in the past lives, you have already accomplished a lot. This placement shows that you were a workaholic person and you developed a lot of karma at your workplace.

Your soul has already done a lot of work in past life and therefore it does not want to experience work again in this life. It has a desire to experience the homely happiness, the luxuries of life, the homely life. But your soul has incarnated as a human being and you have to work in this life as well, so you're not happy while working because that is not the requirement of your soul. It wants to experience the luxuries of life, the happiness of life, and it becomes very difficult when you have to work even though you are least interested. It seems like an obligation on you but you cannot escape the karmas in this life.

People with Ketu in the 10th house of horoscope have the responsibility to understand that life is not about luxury no matter what kind of work you have done in the past life. You have to work if you are on Earth. Without karma, there is no fruit. This makes life very difficult when you want to stay at home and enjoy life but life is demanding work from you. It's a kind of a difficult situation. People with such placement of Ketu should understand that without working life will not move forward so the best way for them is to work in such a way that they do not get bored because such people tend to get bored with one kind of work so they should take such a work in which there is a movement or they don't have to stick to one type of work or place. In this way, it will be easy to survive as well. Else you can start one kind of work and when it runs you can give the responsibility to others and then you can take the other kind of responsibility for yourself. Never stick to one kind of work when Ketu is there in the tenth house otherwise you can feel that life is so boring and that will create a lot of stress in your heart and anxiety in your brain.

The most important lesson of life for these people is that they can change work, but should not leave any work incomplete. They should never give up on their duties. Never give up on their work because this is their karmic debt from their past life. In the past, they might have not fulfilled their responsibility and other people may have suffered because of them. So it is the moral responsibility of such individuals not to run away from work. Do it with full heart and concentration.

Ketu in the Eleventh House

...

Let's understand the eleventh house before talking about the effects of Ketu in it.

The eleventh house has the following attributes:-

1- Fulfilment of desires.

2- Profit & Gains.

3- Social network.

4- Friend circle.

5- Elder siblings.

Ketu in the 11th house brings a past life karmic knot related to the attributes of this house.

It brings a possibility that you are not attached to your friends, elder siblings, etc. Either they are missing from your life and even if they are present then a point will come when you will have to face a challenging situation related to them and you might get completely detached from them. That perfect kind of bond is missing among friends /social circle / with elder siblings.

If you want to grow further in life then you must learn to let go. You must not fall into the trap of fulfilment of desires otherwise you will have to face lots of emotional traumas and emotional dissatisfaction.

Rather, stay detached from all the attributes of the eleventh house, and then you will see how beautifully your desires will be fulfilled.

Ketu here indicates that you have already lived a life full of social networking in the past.

You were too focused on profits and gains but now is the time to understand love and emotions.

You need to understand that life is not only about gains. Learn to appreciate the more emotional and creative aspects of life.

Ketu in the Twelfth House

...

12 house is where Ketu feels the most comfort and has the power to take you towards salvation or moksha. But this is only possible if you are aligned with Ketu. Otherwise, it will not let you sleep and will create too much restlessness in your life.

12th house represents the following:-

1- Spiritual world .

2- Foreign land.

3- Hospitals.

4- Jail, Imprisonment.

5- Investment.

6- Expenses and Losses.

7- Bed pleasure.

8. Dreams.

9. Ghost/spirits/souls/ancestors(Pitra)

Ketu in the twelfth house is like a saint in you. In previous life, you had reached a place where you had experienced all life processes. You were on the path of spirituality but then you had also developed certain karmas on that path. You might have taken a shortcut and directly entered the spiritual path but didn't express selfless service towards society. Hence this life is giving you the chance to understand that unless you provide services to mankind and society, the journey is not complete.

Ketu in the twelfth house is about being spiritual, but still not being actively involved in it. This placement can make you highly intuitive as your spiritual practices like meditation in past life are carried forward in this birth as your intuition. With this placement of Ketu in the birth chart it is always good if you are involved in practices like yoga, meditation, and donations as it will help you to grow further in life.

You must pay attention to your dreams as you are connected to other world(soul world) in your sleep and there is a possibility that Ketu will help you bring messages for you through dreams.

Rahu and Your Present Life

...

Talking about Ketu was about our roots, our past life, and our karmic knot but life is not only about our deeds in the past, it is about our present as well.

Whatever is done can't be undone but can only be rectified to an extent. But what we can gain further is through our present.

Our present can help us grow. It can help us move forward and build a strong future.

Our present is going to be the past of our coming future so the importance of the present is the most.

Rahu represents our present life. What all desires our soul has that it needs to fulfil are deeply seeded in Rahu. If Ketu holds the information of the past then Rahu holds the key to the present life.

Whatever our soul could not accomplish in the past it is looking forward to achieving in the present through Rahu. Ignoring Rahu is like living in ignorance of the present and thereby destroying your future.

To understand what Rahu has in store for you in this birth that you need to unlock, you first have to understand what exactly Rahu is.

Rahu as a planet in astrology is about:

1- Obsession
2- Illusion
3- Passion
4- Head of Kundalini serpent
5- Crown chakra
6- Head
7- Unlimited expansion
8- Foreign element
9- Unorthodox
10- Desires
11- Limitless
12- Uncertainty
13- Unsatisfied
14- Greedy
15- Unethical
16- Selfishness
17- Lust
18- Unstable
19- Unpredictable

What is that we will be running after in this life subconsciously are the unfulfilled desires from our past life. Wherever Rahu is placed in your birth chart you need to understand it very deeply as you may be obsessed with that energy. Rahu can take you away from reality by creating an illusion and you might lose everything rather than gain. If obsession takes over you then you will keep running after that desire endlessly and you might land up in frustration if the path chosen is not correct.

We need to understand the energy of Rahu in our lives as it will pave the way for our souls to grow.

Let us understand what role Rahu plays in different houses of birth chart or horoscope.

Rahu in the First House

...

When Rahu energy is placed in the first house of the horoscope then it is very clear that the person is self-obsessed.

The first house is -self, personality, and outer appearance.

So Rahu here will make you focused on yourself and such a person is least bothered about her/his partner or other people.

There is a probability that you might be over-obsessed about yourself and might feel that you are the best and wherever you go you should be accepted as the best.

You might be focused on how you look and will take great care of your dress, appearance, etc.

When Rahu is placed in the first house you must understand that taking care of yourself is good but when you overdo it and ignore others around you then you might face lots of issues, especially in relationships with others especially with your life partner, your family life can get destroyed. You might end up alone as people will start running away from you because you think only about yourself and such personalities are not liked by anyone.

With Rahu in the first house, you want personality expansion and want to be the centre of attraction no matter what. But that's not always possible. So a time comes when frustration develops. In the past life, you lived for others but in this life, you have desires to live for yourself that make you self-centred. What you need to understand is that you need to control this self-centredness and be a genuine part of others as well.

With Rahu in the first house, there is an axis of the first and seventh house that is you and your life partner or your business partner. You should always try to create a balance between you and the other person. Try to control the selfish attitude because Rahu is here to experience self and Rahu is an illusion creator. So be very aware that taking care of yourself does not mean that you have to neglect others. Do not fall into the illusion created by Rahu that you are the best and others are nothing in front of you.

Rahu in the Second House

...

The second house is about the following:-

1-Food habits and our taste

2-Speech

3-Family

4-Our immediate family

5-Our liquid assets that are saved in our banks

When Rahu is placed in the second house of your birth chart it can make you a person who has the desire to have a good amount of money in the bank. But Rahu is a very unstable planet. So your bank account can be in waves of ups and downs. Depending upon the sign(zodiac) it is placed in, sometimes your bank can overflow with money and sometimes there is a scarcity, but your focus is money. This placement of Rahu can also make you a lover of different varieties of food and it is difficult for such people to control their eating habits.

In a way, their eating habits can be the root cause of their health problems.

Rahu is a foreign element. So people with Rahu in the second house of the horoscope can be fluent in languages other than their mother tongue. Also, they can use their voice for the expansion of their life. For example, singers with Rahu in their second house can sing very well as Rahu can help them in creating variation in their voice texture. They can also be good orators, they might speak very fast when required. All you need to understand is to take care of the attributes of the second house when Rahu is there and not overdo it else you might land up in trouble.

The family environment may not be very cordial when such people are born.

Rahu in the Third House

...

The third house represents the following:-

1- Efforts

2- Younger siblings

3- Social media

4- Communication

5- Short trips through roads

6- Office colleagues

7- Relatives

8- Neighbours

9- Office environment

10- Publications

With Rahu's placement in the third house of the birth chart, the person is smart enough to make the right efforts. Such people tend to over-communicate sometimes and others may not like it. So be aware of your communication. Generally, it is seen that such people tend to accomplish their goal by hook or by crook just like Rahu, and want to use their brains more than using physical labour when it comes to efforts.

There is a possibility that such individuals are obsessed with their younger siblings.

This is Kalyug, a period of machines, computers, etc. So placement of Rahu in the third house is a good placement. Nowadays it can help you accomplish tasks through the means of machines and computers. One can be very proficient while using electronic gadgets, this placement can help one in growing through social media platforms.

Rahu is brain so being sharp at mind and using your brain in your efforts can help you achieve anything in life. But remember that overusing of brain can harm as well. You need to use your physical body as well. So don't be a lazy person. Use your physical body as well.

This placement of Rahu can make you a talkative person but help yourself to work on your communication skills to get the best results through this placement of Rahu.

Rahu is an expansion so if you choose to grow through publications then it can help you.

The only way to use the positive side of this planet is by avoiding overindulgence and obsession with anything. Try to create a balanced energy. Also, learn to differentiate between illusion and reality related to second house attributes because Rahu is very good at creating illusion.

Rahu in the Fourth House

...

The fourth house is all about the following:-

1-Mother

2-Motherland

3-Homely happiness

4-Happiness of heart

5-Immovable assets, property, vehicles,

6-Educational institute and much more.

An unsatisfied planet in the house of happiness and satisfaction ,will always make you uneasy as you will keep running after happiness but this search is going to be never-ending. Nothing will make you satisfied. When one of your desire will get fulfilled your focus will shift to another desire and so on. Hence meditation is a must for people with Rahu in their fourth house and there is a need to limit your desires. Otherwise, Rahu's unsatisfied energy will make your heart filled with grief and sorrow even after achieving a lot.

People with Rahu in the fourth house always desire to have a luxurious life with branded vehicles, big houses, and so on.

There is an obsession with luxuries in life. There is also an obsession with their mother when Rahu is placed here.

There might be an urge to settle in a foreign country as Rahu is a foreign element in the house of motherland.

Such people are not fond of the traditional way of the education system and may look for an alternative way of education or conditions in their life and they may change many schools during basic education, depending on the transits and Dasha.

When Rahu is in the fourth house of the birth chart, you must understand that in your previous life, you did not get a chance to stay at home or enjoy homely happiness as you may have been busy in the outer world or you were doing work most of the time. So in this life, your soul wants to experience home. All the attributes of the fourth house were missing in past life and your soul wants to experience all the attributes of the fourth house in this life.

Try to keep a balance between work and home and then only real happiness will be achieved. Otherwise, you might end up living a very unsatisfied life.

Rahu in Fifth House

...

The fifth house represents the following:-

1-Creativity

2-Romance, love affairs, emotions

3-Children

4-Intellect

5-Entertainment and films

6-Education

7-Intelligence, etc.

When Rahu is placed in the house of creativity it can make you a highly creative person and very intelligent. Your IQ level can be very high. If you are in the film industry, Rahu can make you a superstar as Rahu is expansion.

It creates an obsession for the children, but because it is a foreign element it might indicate conceiving through alternative methods like IVF, surrogacy, adoption, etc. But that also depends on the placement of other planets as well as the Rashi (zodiac) in which Rahu is placed.

When it comes to love, This placement can give you many romantic relationships as Rahu is an unsatisfied energy and it might give you dissatisfaction in love and such a person moves on in search of satisfaction from one person to another. It can also create an illusion that someone better is there for you. That is why it creates instability in love life and the probability of having more than one romantic relation can be seen if the horoscope is supporting it.

With Rahu in the fifth house, you must understand that there is nothing like perfect in this world and you have to control your emotions else you will invite a lot of dissatisfaction in your love life.

You are born to experience the attributes of the fifth house. In this life, you are born to experience love but remember life is not a bed of roses. So whatever we are here to experience, it is for sure that we will have to face problems regarding those attributes. So instead of running after everything try to maintain a balance and create an equilibrium in your life as this is very important to learn in this life to grow as a soul.

Rahu in the Sixth House

...

The sixth house is a very happening and interesting placement when it comes to Rahu. This house is about:-

1-Short term Disease

2-Hidden enemies

3-litigations & Court cases

4-Loans, debts

5-Accumulated karmas of the past life

6-Challenges, competitions, day-to-day struggles in life, etc.

When a planet of illusion and confusion is sitting here, the right diagnosis of disease is difficult. No matter how efficient the doctor is Rahu can create an illusion when it comes to diagnosis. So the patient with such placement must be very careful before starting any kind of medical treatment. Allopathic treatment doesn't go well for such people and it is recommended to look for some alternative therapies for treatment because Rahu is not about roots. It is about foreign techniques. So whichever technique is prevalent in the society during that period, Rahu would like to take some other path.

Secondly, this placement of Rahu gives lots of hidden enemies. But it also makes the person sharp enough to handle the enemies very well. Rahu is brain, generally these people will never handle enemies head-on or manually rather their approach will be mysterious and diplomatic.

Rahu is an unlimited expansion, so people with this placement of Rahu should be cautious while taking loans as it might keep them in loans for long or can create a never ending loan cycle in life.

Rahu in the sixth house knows how to handle any kind of struggle, although it expands the struggles in life.

Opposite to the sixth house is the 12th house which is the house of salvation. So Rahu in the sixth house can help you understand the struggles of life so that you can approach moksha. Although it is one of the best placements of Rahu but get ready to lead a life filled with challenges. One has to understand that crossing the challenges of life can only help you win and attain salvation. Rahu's placement in the sixth house can help you through the process of challenges, as you are born to experience the challenges in this life. You may have lived a life of loneliness and stayed far away from any kind of struggle. In this life, you are here to experience day-to-day challenges of life.

Rahu in the Seventh House

...

Each coin has two faces, bright and dark. Rahu placed in the seventh house of your birth chart is an indication that you have a desire to experience partnership in this life. In the previous birth, you were completely focused on yourself and now you have an urge to live for others. The never-ending expansion of Rahu in the seventh house can disturb your married life as you will never feel satisfied with your partner and you might feel that you will get a better person than the existing one. But one must understand that it is an illusion created by Rahu. So people with seventh house Rahu should try to handle their life partner and must try to stabilize their married life otherwise it will make your life full of instability. Seventh houses is about mass, public, and business. The bright side of Rahu here can make you a good sales person as you will have good qualities to handle people for selling things so it can expand your business.

The seventh house is about :

1-Life partner

2-Business partner

3-Business

4-Any kind of legal partnership

In all the above attributes, Rahu can make you obsessed, a person can have more than one partner, can be obsessed with business and can work in the direction of business expansion, especially in foreign lands.

How do you want to handle the energy of Rahu in the seventh house is up to you. It can give you lots of dissatisfaction in the partnership or it can help you to take care of your partner like no one else can, thereby making your life happy. This energy in the seventh house can help you to connect with more and more people. If you are interested in politics, then Rahu sitting here can help you connect with the masses. You will be able to handle them through your intelligence because Rahu is very intelligent if used properly. Otherwise, Rahu can create an illusion that can harm you.

Rahu in the Eighth House

...

The eighth house is the house of the unknown mysteries and the planet of mysteries here can do a lot for you. But only if handled properly otherwise it can make you very troublesome.

Let's understand what is Eighth house about. It represents the following:-

1- Obstacles

2- Sudden loss and sudden gains

3- In-laws

4- Inheritance

5- Tax department

6- Insurance

7- Occult, Research

8- Hidden and unknown things, Scandals

9- Transformation

10- Death, Longevity

Rahu here can make you do well in a research field. This placement can be very challenging, Rahu is an unexpected energy and this house itself is a house of sudden happenings & unexpected things in life. So there is a possibility that unexpected and sudden events can become a part of your life that will lead to many transformations in your life.

It can make you do many hidden activities but it can also help you explore hidden activities. It all depends on how you handle this energy here. Rahu here wants to experience the mysteries and occult. It can help you in research but if you do not handle this energy properly then it may take you to the wrong path as the eighth house is also the house of a bribe or money earned under the table, so be aware as it may land you up in scandals.

Rahu is a boundless planet so it will not let you follow the traditions of your in-laws but you are here to experience the eighth house in life. So challenges will be coming through this house energy. Although Rahu is an obsession, it can make you obsessed with the attributes of the house but be ready for any kind of sudden happening in your life.

Rahu in Ninth House

...

Let's understand the ninth house first. It is all about the following:-

1-Religion and Dharma

2-Life philosophy

3-Gurus and teachers

4-Religious travel or Dharmic yatra

5-Father

6-Higher studies

7-Wisdom and Luck.

Rahu placed in the house of religious activities and Dharma can make you a person who has an obsession with religious travels. Although Rahu is an unorthodox energy you will have an obsession for the religion but you will not be a follower of religion through orthodox means or traditions. You will be very liberal in the way you follow your religion and also the probability of getting connected with people of different religions is prominent. Ninth house is the house of Guru so if your horoscope allows then you can also be a Guru related to religion or you may meet many gurus in your lifetime.

When Rahu is placed in the ninth house, the house of philosophy, then it can make you a person whose internal belief system is something different from what is portrayed to the outer world.

Rahu does not mind accepting or visiting religious places of other religions because it is an unorthodox planet.

It is a house of wisdom and Rahu is intelligence so sometimes it can create an Illusion and you might not be able to differentiate between good and bad. There is a possibility that your wisdom can be covered with illusion created by this planet. So be very cautious when you are choosing your teacher or Dharma Guru(religious teacher).

Rahu in the Tenth House

...

Before talking about Rahu in the 10th house, let's understand what the 10th house talks about.

1- Outer world, space in the world outside the home where we deal with others

2- A house of profession, career

3- What title do we hold in this world

When Rahu is placed in the house of career, it is for sure that we are here in this world to experience the work and outer world, and we are not here to experience homely happiness.

Our focus is on career and the world outside home because in the past life, our soul has already experienced what is home and how it feels to be in a homely life. So in this life, there is an urge to experience how it is to be in a life that is outside the home.

Rahu is expansion so there is a possibility that such individuals have multiple work fields. Rahu is dissatisfaction so the Probability is, that the person is not satisfied with work and is seeking something more beneficial.

Rahu is instability so it can create instability in the career or profession of such a person.

People with this placement never get satisfied with work and they want to work till the time they are alive and they are always working to create a distinct place for them in this world.

Creating a powerful name in the outside world is what Rahu is looking for.

There can be so many challenges in the world outside for such people.

It is always recommended that when Rahu is placed here such a person should learn to create harmony and balance between home and work. The greed to work and get name and fame sometimes leads to irresponsible behaviour towards home. This life is about learning and learning is always through experience. Rahu is about experiencing this life. So experience the outer world, the profession, and your career but do not forget that your home is also your responsibility.

Rahu in the Eleventh House

...

The eleventh house is regarded as the house of Rahu. This energy feels very happy here because the eleventh house is all about:-

1-fulfillment of desires

2-Profit and gains

3-Friend circle,

4-Social network and

5-Elder siblings.

Rahu's energy is about desires and the eleventh house can fulfil the desires. When Rahu is placed here it is completely focused on fulfilling one's desires, always thinking about profits and gains, creating a huge social network.

A planet of expansion in the house of expansion, a planet of materialism in the house of material desires.

People with Rahu in the eleventh house are always focused on how they can expand their social network, how they can expand their friend circle, how can they get gains and how can they fulfil their desires.

But remember Rahu is also an illusion. It can put you in an illusion of false desires. It will not let you differentiate the practical aspect of life and can create impractical or excessive desires within you. You will not be able to differentiate what is good for you, and what is the real meaning of fulfilment of desires, and throughout your life, you might keep running towards something that is never ending as your desires will never be fulfilled because they are limitless.

Learn to limit your desires when Rahu is placed in the eleventh house of your birth chart.

Try to look for friends who are real and not just superficial because the friend circle you will get through Rahu will be huge but also a kind of illusion and not real friends.

Rahu in the Twelfth House

...

Before talking about how the energy of Rahu works in the twelfth house, let's understand the attributes of this house.

It is about:-

1-Spirituality & Meditation

2-Donation

3-Far away from home, foreign land

4-Hospitals and Prisons

5-Losses

6-Investments and Expenses

7-Sleep etc.

Rahu is superficial therefore sometimes people with Rahu in the house of spirituality might try to deceive people in the name of spirituality and meditation. Such people are not deeply rooted in the spiritual world but portray themselves as highly spiritual and deep meditators.

If you have Rahu in the twelfth house it is highly recommended to do meditations and yoga and try to connect with the universe because Rahu also represents crown Chakra and if you focus the energy of Rahu in the right direction, it can create wonders for you and make you connect to the universe through meditations.

It is all about how you handle the energy of Rahu in the twelfth house.

You can have an obsession to go and settle in foreign lands because it is the house of foreign land and Rahu is an obsession.

Avoid any kind of illegal activities. Otherwise, Rahu can lead to imprisonment.

Take care of your health otherwise visiting the hospital for treatment can become a daily routine. Try to control your expenditures as Rahu can make you lose a lot of money from your pocket on unnecessary things. Rahu when channelised properly through meditations can bring psychic information through dreams.

Such a placement is also responsible for paranormal activities like seeing a soul of dead people.

Conclusion

...

Our journey is a series of many lives. Our soul keeps coming to Earth again and again until it understands its true purpose and becomes capable of going back to its root, which is the ultimate home so that it can reunite with its highest energy from where it has been generated.

In the series of birth and rebirth, how much time it will take to finish up the soul's journey is determined by the decisions that it makes when it is present in a physical body during its lifetime.

Every time the soul incarnates as a human body, it has some important lessons to learn, and it also carries certain baggage from the past, which it needs to shed and that is done by facing struggles and overcoming those challenges and creating new karmas in this birth and taking them to the next level.

Ketu, the South note of the moon is about the roots of the soul in the past life journeys, and thereby the baggage of our deeds from the past. So we cannot ignore Ketu as it can help you grow in this birth by shedding that baggage. On the other hand Rahu, the North Node of Moon is coming with lots of desires to experience in this material world. By handling Rahu and Ketu carefully one can grow tremendously on its soul path.

" Man is the maker of his destiny. "

Learn from the mistakes of the past, rectify them, and create new good karmas for the next life. If you balance the energy of these planets, life will become a beautiful journey full of hope and happiness.

Meditation and the right way of living can help in balancing the energies of Rahu and Ketu.

Ketu is an inward journey, and Rahu is an outward journey.

Balance the two and enjoy the sweetness of life.

www.ingramcontent.com/pod-product-compliance
Lightning Source LLC
LaVergne TN
LVHW061621070526
838199LV00078B/7375